Look at this woman. She is sad. She wants a child but she cannot have one.

One day, she visits a fairy. She asks the fairy for help. The fairy gives her a seed.

The woman is happy. She goes home and she plants the seed. It grows and grows and grows.

Suddenly, a beautiful flower grows.

It opens and there is a small girl.

My beautiful daughter! Your name's Thumbelina.

4

Thumbelina is small but very beautiful. At night, she sleeps in a shell next to the window.

One night, an ugly green toad comes to the window. He takes Thumbelina. She is scared.

Help!

The toad wants to marry Thumbelina but she does not like the ugly toad.

Thumbelina is sad.
She wants to go home.

The fish under the water
want to help her.

The fish swim and swim. Thumbelina sees beautiful places. She is happy!

Bye bye, ugly toad!

The insect leaves Thumbelina
under the trees and flies away.

Now she is cold and very scared.

Suddenly, Thumbelina sees a bird. It is not moving. It is cold. She puts her coat over it.

In the morning, the bird is okay. Thumbelina and the bird fly over the trees. They are happy.

Look! Flowers!

A big white flower opens and there is a prince. He looks at Thumbelina.

You're beautiful. Marry me!

Yes!

Activities

Before You Read

1 Look at the pictures. Read and match.

a fairy   a prince   a girl   a bird   a mother

After You Read

1 Look and say *Good* or *Bad* about the story.

2 Read and say *Yes* or *No*.

a   The fairy gives the mother an apple.

b   At night Thumbelina sleeps in a shell.

c   Thumbelina is ugly.

d   A bird helps Thumbelina.

e   Thumbelina marries the toad.

Pearson Education Limited
Edinburgh Gate, Harlow,
Essex CM20 2JE, England
and Associated Companies throughout the world.

ISBN: 978-1-4082-8830-6

This edition first published by Pearson Education Ltd 2014

1 3 5 7 9 10 8 6 4 2

Set in 17/21pt OT Fiendstar
Printed in China (GCC/01)

Illustrations: Sue Mason

Published by Pearson Education Ltd in association with
Penguin Books Ltd, a Penguin Random House company.

For a complete list of the titles available in the Penguin Kids series please go to www.penguinreaders.com.
Alternatively, write to your local Pearson Education office or to: Penguin Readers Marketing Department,
Pearson Education, Edinburgh Gate, Harlow, Essex CM20 2JE, England.